Mexican Cookbook:

Traditional Mexican Recipes Made Easy

www.grizzlypublishing.com

Introduction

I would like to thank you for purchasing the book "Mexican Cookbook: Traditional Mexican Recipes Made Easy."

Did you know that cooking Mexican food at home could be quite easy? Yes, it can be quite easy, if you are armed with the right cookbook. If you want to learn to cook traditional Mexican recipes like a pro, then this is the right book for you.

Mexican cuisine is one of the most popular cuisines in the world today, just like Asian, Italian and French cuisine. Mexican cuisine is nothing less than a work of art. Mexican recipes are unique, creative, flavorful and extremely delicious.

What is the first thing that comes to your mind when you think about Mexican food? You perhaps think about images of food topped with lots of cheese, fried items and complex sauces. Or you might think about spicy food that makes you sweat! Well, if that's what you think, then you are certainly mistaken. Mexican food is quite simple and fresh.

Most of the Mexican dishes incorporate local produce and grains. The most important aspect of Mexican cooking is that it can perfectly fit into your everyday cooking schedule and it uses only a handful of ingredients. Mexican food doesn't require any fancy produce and you can cook delicious and nutritious meals with only a couple of ingredients. Mexican cuisine is popular for its distinct and bold flavors. Within this cookbook, you will find traditional Mexican recipes like burritos, paella, quesadillas, guacamole, enchiladas and much more. Mexican home cooking can be fun, quick and easy! This book will certainly change your opinion about traditional Mexican cooking within no time. The recipes mentioned in this book are easy to understand, quick to prepare and need minimal ingredients. You can easily procure the ingredients that you need from your local supermarket.

The next time you have your friends or family over for a meal, you can cook tasty and authentic Mexican food for them that will definitely blow their minds! If you want to cook like a pro within no time, then this is the best book for you! With this cookbook, you can learn to cook delicious Mexican recipes, regardless of your level of expertise. You will certainly have fun while cooking these recipes and this simple cookbook will take you on a food voyage like none other. You don't have to stick to the recipes given in this book alone. Once you understand the basic flavor combinations of Mexican food, you can experiment as much as you want.

So, if you are ready to step into the flavorful world of Mexican cuisine, then let us get started without further ado.

Table of Contents

Chapter One: Breakfast Recipes

Mexican Breakfast Quesadilla

Serves: 12

Nutritional values per serving:

Calories – 189, Fat – 11 g, Carbohydrate – 12 g, Protein – 9 g

Ingredients:

- 8 eggs
- 2 small tomatoes, chopped
- ½ teaspoon taco seasoning
- Salt to taste
- Pepper powder to taste
- 2 tablespoons half and half
- 4 slices ham, cubed
- 1 cup cheese, shredded
- 1 teaspoon cooking oil

For avocado salsa:

- 4 medium tomatoes, cubed
- Salt to taste
- Pepper to taste
- A handful cilantro (optional)
- 1 ripe avocado, peeled, pitted chopped
- Salt to taste
- Pepper powder to taste

To serve:

- 6 tortillas
- Sour cream (optional)

- 1 ½ teaspoons oil

Method:

1. Add eggs and half and half into a bowl and whisk well.
2. Place a skillet over medium high heat. Add 2 teaspoons oil. When the oil is heated, add tomatoes and ham and heat thoroughly.
3. Add egg and stir. Cook until the eggs are soft and set. Stir frequently.
4. Turn off the heat and cool for a few minutes.
5. Place tortillas on your countertop. Divide the scramble between the tortillas and place it on one half of the tortilla. Sprinkle cheese over it. Fold the other half over the filling.
6. Place a skillet over medium heat. Add ½ teaspoon oil. When the oil is heated, place the filled quesadillas over it.
7. Cook until the underside is golden brown and crisp. Flip sides and cook the other side until golden brown and crisp.
8. Meanwhile, make the avocado salsa as follows: Add tomato, salt, pepper, avocado and cilantro into a bowl and stir. Cover and set aside for a while for the flavors to set in.
9. Cut each into quesadilla into 2 halves. Drizzle some sour cream on top if using and serve with salsa.

Breakfast Tortas

Serves: 2

Nutritional values per serving: 1 ciabatta roll (2 halves)

Calories – 677, Fat – 24 g, Carbohydrate – 94 g, Protein – 28 g

Ingredients:

- 2 ciabatta rolls
- 3 tablespoons sour cream
- 1 teaspoon lime juice
- Salt to taste
- ¼ cup Monterey Jack cheese
- 2 cooked bacon strips, halved
- ¼ cup salsa
- 6 tablespoons refried black beans
- 2 tablespoons fresh cilantro, minced
- A dash of chipotle hot pepper sauce
- 2 large eggs
- ½ teaspoon olive oil
- ¼ medium ripe avocado, peeled, sliced
- 1 green onion, chopped

Method:

1. Cut each roll into 2 horizontally, at the top third part. Scoop out some of the bread from the bottom part of the rolls and use in another recipe. Set aside bottom part the ciabatta rolls on a baking sheet. Do not grease the baking sheet.
2. Add beans, cilantro, sour cream, lime juice, salt and hot pepper sauce into a bowl and stir.

3. Spoon about 4 tablespoons of the bean mixture in the bottom part of the roll. Crack an egg over the bean mixture.
4. Place the baking sheet in the oven.
5. Bake in a preheated oven at 400° F for 10 minutes. Sprinkle cheese. Brush olive oil on the cut part of the top part of the roll and place on the baking sheet adjacent to the bottom part of the rolls. Bake until the eggs are set.
6. Place bacon, avocado slices and onion. Spoon some salsa on top. Cover with the top part of the rolls.
7. Serve.

Sunrise Sausage Enchiladas

Serves: 5

Nutritional values per serving: 1 enchilada

Calories – 398, Fat – 25 g, Carbohydrate – 30 g, Protein – 14 g

Ingredients:

- ½ pound Jones no sugar Pork sausage roll
- 3 ½ cups frozen shredded hash brown potatoes, thawed (10 ounces)
- ¼ teaspoon chili powder
- Pepper powder to taste
- 1 cup cheddar cheese, shredded, divided
- 1 can (10 ounces) green enchilada sauce
- 1 tablespoon canola oil
- ¼ teaspoon salt or to taste
- Cayenne pepper to taste
- 2 ounces canned chopped green chili
- 5 flour tortillas (6 inches)

For optional toppings:
- Sweet red pepper, chopped
- Red onion, chopped
- Fresh cilantro, chopped

Method:

1. Place a skillet over medium heat. Add sausage and cook until it is not pink anymore. Break it simultaneously as it cooks. Remove sausage with a slotted spoon and set aside on a plate lined with paper towels. Discard the fat remaining in the pan.

2. Place the skillet back over medium high heat. Add potatoes and cook until light brown. Turn off the heat. Add salt, pepper, ¼ cup cheese, sausage, chili powder and cayenne pepper and mix well.
3. Spread the tortillas on your countertop. Place ½ cup of the sausage mixture and spread it along the diameter of the tortilla. Roll and place with its seam side facing down in a greased baking dish.
4. Pour enchilada sauce over the tortilla rolls. Chill for 4-8 hours.
5. Remove the baking dish from the oven 15 minutes before baking. Cover the dish with foil.
6. Bake in a preheated oven at 375° F for 20-25 minutes. Sprinkle remaining cheese on top.
7. Remove the foil and bake for some more time until the cheese melts. Sprinkle the optional toppings if using and serve.

Chorizo & Grits Breakfast Bowls

Serves: 3

Nutritional values per serving:

Calories – 344, Fat – 14 g, Carbohydrate – 30 g, Protein – 24 g

Ingredients:

- 1 teaspoon olive oil
- 1 medium zucchini, chopped
- 6 tablespoons quick cooking grits
- ¼ cup cheddar cheese, shredded
- Pico de Gallo to serve (optional)
- A handful fresh cilantro, chopped to serve (optional)
- 6 ounces fully cooked chorizo chicken sausages, sliced
- 1 ½ cups water
- 7.5 ounces black beans, rinsed, drained
- 3 large eggs

Method:

1. Place a nonstick skillet over medium heat. Add oil. When the oil is heated, stir in the sausage and sauté until light brown.
2. Stir in the zucchini and sauté until tender. Transfer into a bowl and keep warm in an oven.
3. Add water into a saucepan. Place the saucepan over medium heat. When it begins to boil, add grits slowly and stir.
4. Lower the heat to medium low. Cover with a lid. Let it simmer until thick. Stir occasionally.
5. Add beans and cheese and mix well. Turn off the heat.

6. Clean the skillet and place it back over medium heat. When the skillet is heated, spray with cooking spray. Cook the eggs, sunny side up.
7. To assemble: Divide the grits into 3 serving bowls. Divide the chorizo mixture and place over the grits. Place an egg on top.
8. Top with Pico de Gallo and cilantro if using and serve.

Tomatillo Breakfast Tacos

Serves: 4

Nutritional values per serving: 2 tacos

Calories – 418, Fat – 24 g, Carbohydrate – 32 g, Protein – 20 g

Ingredients:

- 2 tablespoons extra-virgin olive oil
- ½ cup onions
- 8 large eggs, lightly beaten
- Salt to taste
- Black pepper powder to taste
- 8 small corn tortillas (4-5 inches each)
- 16 ounces medium tomatillos, husked, rinsed, chopped
- 4 cloves garlic, peeled, minced
- ½ cup queso Blanco or feta cheese

Method:

1. Place a large nonstick skillet over medium heat. Add oil. When the oil is heated, add onion, garlic and tomatillos and sauté until nearly dry.
2. Whisk together eggs, salt and pepper in a bowl. Pour into the skillet. Stir frequently and cook until the eggs are set.
3. Warm the tortillas following the instructions on the package.

4. Spread the tortillas on a serving platter or on individual serving plates.
5. Divide the tomatillo mixture over the tortillas. Sprinkle cheese on top.
6. Serve right away.

Huevos Rancheros Verdes

Serves: 2

Nutritional values per serving: 1 Huevos Rancheros Verdes

Calories – 424, Fat – 20 g, Carbohydrate – 42 g, Protein – 20 g

Ingredients:

- ¾ cup romaine lettuce, thinly sliced
- A handful fresh cilantro, chopped
- 1 teaspoon lime juice
- Freshly ground black pepper to taste
- ¼ cup prepared green salsa
- Canola oil cooking spray
- 2 large eggs
- 1 small scallion, sliced
- 1 ½ teaspoons canola oil, divided
- Salt to taste
- 7.5 ounces canned pinto beans, rinsed
- 4 corn tortillas (6 inches each)
- 6 tablespoons shredded sharp cheddar cheese

Method:

1. Add beans and salsa into a bowl and stir.
2. Add lettuce, cilantro, scallion, salt, pepper, lime juice and ½ teaspoon oil into another bowl and stir.
3. Spray tortillas with cooking spray and place on a large baking sheet in 2 sets of overlapping pairs (the tortillas in 1 set should overlap each other by about 3 inches).
4. Spread a layer of half the bean mixture on the top of each set of tortillas.

5. Scatter half the cheese on each set.
6. Bake in a preheated oven at 400° F until the beans are heated and the cheese melts.
7. Place a nonstick pan over medium heat. Cook the eggs, sunny side up with the remaining oil. Sprinkle salt and pepper.
8. Serve the tortilla sets in individual serving plates. Place an egg over each set. Divide the lettuce mixture and place around the egg and serve.

Mexican Potato Omelet

Serves: 1

Nutritional values per serving:

Calories – 335, Fat – 23 g, Carbohydrate – 11 g, Protein – 21 g

Ingredients:

- 1 teaspoon extra-virgin olive oil, divided
- ½ can (from a 4 ½ ounce can) chopped mild green chilies
- ¼ teaspoon hot sauce like Tabasco
- Freshly ground black pepper to taste
- 1 small scallion, chopped
- ½ cup frozen hash brown potatoes or diced cooked potatoes
- 2 large eggs
- Salt to taste
- ¼ cup pepper Jack cheese or cheddar cheese, grated
- A handful fresh cilantro or parsley, chopped

Method:

1. Place an ovenproof nonstick skillet (about 7-8 inches diameter) over medium high heat.
2. Add ½ teaspoon oil. When the oil is heated, add potatoes and sauté until golden brown. Toss every 3-4 minutes.
3. Add chilies and mix well. Remove the potatoes on to a plate.

4. Place rack in the oven, 4 inches from the heating element for broiling. Let the oven preheat.
5. Add eggs, salt, pepper and hot sauce into a bowl and whisk well.
6. Add cheese, cilantro, scallion and potato mixture and mix well.
7. Clean the pan and place over medium heat. Add remaining oil and swirl the pan so that the oil spreads.
8. Add egg mixture into the pan and swirl the pan so that the egg mixture spreads well.
9. Lower heat to low and lift the edges of the omelet on and off for the egg mixture to slide onto the bottom of the pan. Cook for about 2-3 minutes.
10. Transfer the pan into the oven and broil until the omelet is set.
11. Carefully slide the omelet on a plate and serve.

Easy Vegan Breakfast Burritos

Serves: 3

Nutritional values per serving: Without tortillas, only filling

Calories – 202, Fat – 6.25 g, Carbohydrate – 31.8 g, Protein – 5.6 g

Ingredients:

- 1 ½ cups bell pepper, sliced into 2 inches long strips
- ¾ cup cooked chickpeas, drained
- 6 ounces cup red or gold potatoes, cut into ¼ inch pieces
- Salt to taste
- Black pepper powder to taste
- ¾ cup smooth salsa of your choice
- ¾ cup frozen corn, thawed
- ¼ teaspoon ground chipotle chili or more to taste
- ¾ teaspoon ground cumin
- 2 tablespoons water
- 3 large tortillas

For avocado cumin cream:

- 1 medium avocado, peeled, pitted, chopped
- 1 teaspoon water
- 1 ½ tablespoons salsa
- Salt to taste
- 1 jalapeño, chopped
- 1 teaspoon ground cumin

Method:

1. Place the potatoes in a lined baking dish. Sprinkle salt and pepper over the potatoes. Spread it evenly in a single layer.
2. Bake in a preheated oven at 400° F for 20 minutes or until tender.
3. Place a pan over medium heat. Add 2 tablespoons water and bell peppers and cook until dry.
4. Add rest of the ingredients and simmer until the mixture is thick. Turn off the heat.
5. To make avocado cumin cream: Add all the ingredients of avocado cumin cream into a blender and blend until smooth. Add water to dilute if desired.
6. Place the tortillas on your countertop. Spread the vegetable mixture on the tortillas. Spoon in some avocado cumin cream. Wrap like a burrito and serve.

Mexican Migas

Serves: 1

Nutritional values per serving:

Calories – 630, Fat – 38 g, Carbohydrate – 51 g, Protein – 35 g

Ingredients:

- 2 eggs, beaten
- ¼ cup salsa
- 4 sprigs cilantro
- ¾ cup refried beans
- 2 corn tortillas, cut into short strips, preferably stale tortillas
- 2 tablespoons chopped white onion
- 1.5 ounce ranchero cheese
- 3 corn chips
- 1 ½ tablespoons oil

Method:

1. Place a skillet over medium heat. Add oil. When the oil is heated, add tortilla strips and cook until golden brown.
2. Pour egg over the tortillas and do not stir for 50-60 seconds. Stir and cook until the eggs are set. Stir frequently.
3. Add salsa and stir.
4. Transfer into a plate. Sprinkle cheese, cilantro and onion. Place refried beans and corn chips on the side and serve.

Tres Leches Overnight Oats

Serves: 2

Nutritional values per serving: Without toppings

Calories – 408, Fat – 11 g, Carbohydrate – 72 g, Protein – 11 g

Ingredients:

- 1 cup old fashioned rolled oats
- 4 tablespoons sweetened condensed milk
- ½ cup almond milk
- ¼ cup evaporated milk
- ¼ teaspoon ground cinnamon
- 1 banana, sliced
- ¼ cup walnuts, chopped

Method:

1. Divide oats, condensed milk, almond milk, evaporated milk, cinnamon, banana and walnuts equally into 2 containers with a lid.
2. Fasten the lid and shake until well combined.
3. Chill for 7-8 hours and serve with toppings of your choice.

Whole Egg, Bacon and Avocado Quesadilla

Serves: 2

Nutritional values per serving:

Calories – 437, Fat – 32.1 g, Carbohydrate – 16 g, Protein – 22.5 g

Ingredients:

- 1 ½ rashers streaky bacon, chopped
- 2 eggs
- ¼ cup cheese, grated
- 2 flour tortillas
- 1 medium avocado, peeled, pitted, halved, sliced
- Salt to taste
- Pepper to taste

Method:

1. Place a skillet over high heat. Add bacon and cook until the way you like it cooked. Remove bacon with a slotted spoon and place on a plate lined with paper towels.
2. Discard excess fat from the skillet and remove any browned bits that are stuck to the bottom of the skillet.
3. Place the skillet back over medium heat.
4. Place a tortilla on it. Place the avocado slices on one half of the tortilla in a round shape (place them one next to the other until it completes a circle).
5. Crack an egg inside the round in the center (formed by avocado slices).

6. Sprinkle salt, pepper, half the bacon and cheese over it. Fold the other half over the filling. Cook until the underside is golden brown and crisp.
7. Carefully flip sides and cook until the underside is golden brown and crisp. Serve right away.
8. Repeat the steps 3-7 to make the other quesadilla.

Banana Licuado

Serves: 1

Nutritional values per serving:

Calories – 119, Fat – 2.5 g, Carbohydrate – 19.8 g, Protein – 5.2 g

Ingredients:

- 1 cup milk
- 1 tablespoon sugar or to taste
- ½ ripe banana, sliced
- Ice cubes, as required
- Powdered nutmeg to garnish

Method:

1. Add milk, sugar, banana and ice into a blender. Blend for 30-40 seconds or until smooth.
2. Pour into a glass.
3. Sprinkle nutmeg on top and serve.

Horchata Smoothie

Serves: 1

Nutritional values per serving:

Calories – 213, Fat – 8 g, Carbohydrate – 33 g, Protein – 4.4 g

Ingredients:

- ½ cup Horchata
- 2 ice cubes
- 3 Horchata pulp ice cubes
- ¼ banana, sliced, frozen
- ¼ teaspoon vanilla extract
- 1/8 teaspoon ground cinnamon
- 2-3 dates, pitted, chopped
- ¼ teaspoon chai spice mixture

Method:

1. Add Horchata, ice cubes, Horchata pulp ice cubes, banana, vanilla, cinnamon, dates and chai spice mixture into a blender and blend 40-50 seconds or until smooth.
2. Pour into a tall glass and serve.

Mexicali Green Smoothie

Serves: 1

Nutritional values per serving:

Calories – 263, Fat – 8.4 g, Carbohydrate – 50.2 g, Protein – 5.4 g

Ingredients:

- ½ orange, peeled, separated into segments, deseeded
- Juice of ½ large lime
- ½ cup Turkish cucumber
- ½ banana, sliced
- 1 slice jalapeño
- ¼ bunch fresh cilantro, chopped
- ½ cup pineapple chunks
- ¼ avocado, peeled, pitted, chopped
- ½ cup baby kale
- Chia seeds to garnish (optional)
- Water, as required
- Ice cubes, as required

Method:

1. Add orange, lime juice, cucumber, banana, jalapeño, cilantro, pineapple, avocado, kale and a little water into the blender. Blend for 30-40 seconds or until smooth.
2. Pour into a tall glass and serve with ice.

Chapter Two: Lunch Recipes

Soups:

Poblano-Turkey Sausage Chili

Serves: 3

Nutritional values per serving: 1 cup and 2 teaspoons sour cream

Calories – 218, Fat – 3.5 g, Carbohydrate – 25.7 g, Protein – 14.3 g

Ingredients:

- 1 teaspoon canola oil
- ½ tablespoon garlic, peeled, minced
- ½ tablespoon chili powder
- ¼ teaspoon ground cumin
- 2/3 cup unsalted chicken stock, divided
- 7.5 ounces canned pinto beans, rinsed, drained
- 7.5 ounces canned black beans, rinsed, drained
- ¼ cup fresh cilantro, chopped
- 6 teaspoons sour cream
- 4 ounces sweet turkey Italian sausage, discard casing
- ¼ teaspoon dried oregano
- 1 bay leaf
- 1 poblano chili, deseeded, finely chopped
- 1 can (14 ounces) diced tomatoes, with its liquid
- 1 tablespoon all-purpose flour
- Freshly ground pepper to taste
- Radish slices to serve (optional)

Method:

1. Place a Dutch oven over medium high heat. Add oil. When the oil is heated, add garlic and onion and cook until brown.
2. Add sausage, chili powder, cumin, oregano, bay leaf and poblano pepper and mix well. Break meat simultaneously as it cooks. Cook until brown.
3. Add ½ cup stock, both the beans and tomatoes.
4. When it begins to boil, lower the heat and simmer until it is slightly thick.
5. Add remaining stock into a bowl. Add flour and mix well. Pour into the pot. Stir constantly until thick.
6. Turn off the heat. Add cilantro and pepper powder. Remove the bay leaf.
7. Ladle into bowls. Drizzle 2 teaspoons sour cream in each bowl. Place radish slices if desired and serve.

Tortilla Soup with Chorizo and Turkey Meatballs

Serves: 2

Nutritional values per serving:

Calories – 288, Fat – 11.1 g, Carbohydrate – 21.2 g, Protein – 27.4 g

Ingredients:

- 1 teaspoon olive oil
- 6 tablespoons chopped poblano pepper, deseeded
- 2 cups unsalted chicken stock
- 1 corn tortilla, chopped
- ¼ teaspoon garlic powder
- ¼ teaspoon ground coriander
- ¼ teaspoon ground cumin
- ½ cup onion, chopped
- ½ ounce Spanish chorizo, finely chopped
- 6 ounces 93% lean ground turkey
- 7.2 ounces canned diced tomatoes, drained
- Salt to taste
- 1 small egg
- 6 tablespoons frozen corn kernels
- Cooking spray
- A handful fresh cilantro, chopped

Method:

1. Place a saucepan over medium high heat. Add oil. When the oil is heated, stir in the onion, chorizo and poblano and cook for 2 minutes.
2. Stir in the tomatoes and stock. When it begins to boil, lower the heat and add tortillas. Let it simmer.

3. Meanwhile, add ground turkey, all the spices and egg into a bowl and mix well.
4. Divide the mixture into 6 equal portions and shape into balls.
5. Place a nonstick skillet over medium heat. Spray with cooking spray. Place the meatballs in the pan. Cook until brown on all the sides.
6. Drop the meatballs into the simmering soup. Add salt and corn. Cook for 5 more minutes.
7. Ladle into soup bowls. Sprinkle cilantro on top and serve.

Posole (Tomatillo, Chicken, and Hominy Soup)

Serves: 4

Nutritional values per serving:

Calories – 233, Fat – 4.1 g, Carbohydrate – 19.4 g, Protein – 31.8 g

Ingredients:

- ½ pound tomatillos, remove stem and husks
- 1 cup onions, chopped
- 2 cloves garlic, sliced
- 1 can white hominy (15 ounces), drained
- ¼ cup cilantro, chopped
- 4 lime wedges
- 1 ½ pounds chicken breasts, halved, skinned
- 3 cups brown chicken stock
- 1 jalapeño pepper, seeded, quartered
- ½ teaspoon salt or to taste
- 2 tablespoons reduced fat sour cream

Method:

1. Place a pot of water over medium heat. When it begins to boil, add whole tomatillos and cook until tender.
2. Drain and blend the tomatillos until smooth.
3. Place the pot back on heat. Add stock, onions, chicken breasts, garlic, hominy and pepper.
4. When it begins to boil, lower heat and simmer until the chicken is cooked. Remove chicken with a slotted spoon and place on your cutting board. Shred chicken with a pair of forks and discard the bones. Add it back in the pot.

5. Add blended tomatillos and salt. Simmer for 5-7 minutes.
6. Ladle into soup bowls. Garnish with cilantro, sour cream, and lime wedges. Serve hot.

Traditional Mexican Sopa de Fideo

Serves: 2

Nutritional values per serving: 2 cups

Calories – 469, Fat – 17 g, Carbohydrate – 43 g, Protein – 20 g

Ingredients:

- 4 ounces Fideo noodles
- 1 clove garlic, minced
- ½ ripe avocado, peeled, pitted, sliced, to garnish (optional)
- 1 ½ tablespoons vegetable oil
- 1 plum tomato, halved, deseeded
- 1 small white onion, chopped
- 4 cups homemade chicken broth
- Salt to taste

Method:

1. Puree the tomato and set aside.
2. Place a saucepan over medium heat. Add oil. When the oil is heated, add noodles and sauté until it begins to become brown. Some noodles will be browner than the rest.
3. Add blended tomato, garlic and onion and mix until the noodles are well coated.
4. Pour broth and salt and mix well.
5. When it begins to boil, lower heat and cover with a lid. Simmer for 7-8 minutes.
6. Ladle into soup bowls and serve garnished with avocado.

Salads:

Turkey Taco Salad

Serves: 2

Nutritional values per serving:

Calories – 487, Fat – 15 g, Carbohydrate – 54 g, Protein – 39 g

Ingredients:

For salad:

- 1 fajita size flour tortilla, halved, cut into ½ inch strips
- Salt to taste
- ½ pound 93% lean ground turkey
- ½ teaspoon ground cumin
- ½ head romaine lettuce, chopped
- 5.5 ounces canned Mexican style corn, drained
- 1 small ripe avocado, peeled, pitted, chopped
- ¼ cup low fat sharp cheddar cheese, shredded
- 1 teaspoon extra-virgin olive oil, divided
- Pepper powder to taste
- ½ tablespoon chili powder
- ¼ teaspoon garlic powder
- 7.5 ounces canned low sodium black beans, rinsed, drained
- 1 cup cherry tomato, halved
- ½ cup cilantro, chopped
- 1 green onion, thinly sliced
- Cooking spray

- 2 tablespoons plain nonfat Greek yogurt
- 2 tablespoons salsa

Method:

1. Adjust the rack in the center of the oven.
2. Grease a rimmed baking sheet with nonstick cooking spray.
3. Spread the tortilla strips in the center of the baking sheet. Brush with ½ teaspoon oil. Season with salt and pepper. Toss well. Spread it all over the baking sheet, in a single layer.
4. Bake in a preheated oven at 425° F for 8- 10 minutes or until crisp. Flip sides halfway through baking. Remove from the oven and cool. Set aside to garnish.
5. Place a nonstick skillet over medium high heat. Add remaining oil. When the oil is heated, add turkey, garlic powder, pepper, salt, chili powder and cumin powder and mix well.
6. Break the meat simultaneously as it cooks. Cook until the meat is tender.
7. Add salsa and yogurt into a bowl and mix well.
8. Add romaine lettuce into a serving bowl. Add meat mixture and rest of the ingredients. Toss well.
9. Divide into 2 bowls. Top with tortilla strips and serve.

Mexican Street Corn Salad

Serves: 4

Nutritional values per serving: Without serving options

Calories – 181, Fat – 4.6 g, Carbohydrate – 28.6 g, Protein – 8.8 g

Ingredients:

For dressing:

- ¼ cup plain, nonfat yogurt
- ½ teaspoon honey
- A large pinch cumin
- ½ tablespoon lime juice
- ¼ teaspoon paprika

For salad:

- 2 ears corn, shucked, remove kernels (about 1 ½ cups kernels)
- ½ cup canned or cooked black beans, drained, rinsed
- 2 tablespoons extra-virgin olive oil
- 1 small red bell pepper, deseeded, chopped
- ¼ cup cilantro, finely chopped
- 1 large jalapeño chili or to taste, finely sliced
- 1 small red onion, peeled, chopped
- 1 tablespoon lime juice
- 1 small clove garlic, minced
- ¼ cup cotija cheese, shredded
- Sea salt to taste

Method:

1. To make dressing: Add all the ingredients of the dressing into a bowl and whisk well. Cover and set aside for a while for the flavors to set in.

2. Place a nonstick skillet over medium heat. Add oil. When the oil is heated, add garlic and corn and cook until the corn slightly begins to become brown. Stir frequently. Transfer into a bowl.

3. Add lime juice, black beans, onion, cheese, red pepper and cilantro and toss well.

4. Divide salad into serving plates. Divide the dressing and drizzle on top.

5. It can be served cold or warm. You can also serve over tacos or with chips.

Low Carb Taco Salad

Serves: 2

Nutritional values per serving: 2 cups

Calories – 313, Fat – 15 g, Carbohydrate – 16 g, Protein – 32 g

Ingredients:

- 6.4 ounces lean ground beef (85% to 89%)
- 3 green onions, separate the white and green parts, chopped
- 1 small tomato, chopped
- 1 ½ ounces canned olives, sliced
- 3 tablespoons fat free Greek or plain yogurt
- 1 teaspoon chili powder
- 1/3 head romaine lettuce, chopped
- 1/3 avocado, peeled, pitted, chopped
- ½ cup fat free cheese like cheddar or Monterey Jack cheese
- 3 tablespoons salsa

Method:

1. Place a skillet over medium heat. Add beef, white of onion, chili powder, and pepper and salt. Sauté until beef is cooked. Turn off the heat. Cover and set aside if you would like a warm salad or cool completely and chill in the refrigerator if you like chilled salad.
2. Add lettuce, avocado, tomato, greens of the onion and olives into a bowl and toss well. Add the cooked beef and cheese and stir.

3. Divide the salad into serving plates. Drizzle yogurt and salsa on top and serve.

Miscellaneous:

Mexican Vegetarian Quiche

Serves: 4

Nutritional values per serving: 1 wedge

Calories – 273, Fat – 14 g, Carbohydrate – 26 g, Protein – 11 g

Ingredients:

- 6 tablespoons whole wheat flour
- Salt to taste
- 1 tablespoon + 1 teaspoon extra-virgin olive oil
- Salt to taste
- 6 tablespoons corn
- 3 tablespoons pickled jalapeños
- 1 large egg white
- 2 large eggs
- 6 tablespoons low fat milk
- Freshly ground pepper to taste
- 6 tablespoons all-purpose flour
- 1 tablespoon cold butter, chopped into small pieces
- 1-2 tablespoons ice water
- 1 cup onion, chopped
- 1 tablespoon water
- ¼ cup cherry tomatoes, quartered
- ¼ cup Jack cheese, shredded
- 3 tablespoons sour cream

Method:

1. To make crust: Add wheat flour, salt and all-purpose flour into a bowl and mix well.
2. Add butter and mix with your fingers until the butter is well mixed into the flour mixture.
3. Stir in 2 tablespoons sour cream and oil and mix with a fork until well combined.
4. Add iced water and mix until the mixture is soft and well combined. Add a tablespoon of water if necessary. Knead the dough for a couple of minutes.
5. Shape the dough into a circle. Cover the bowl with cling wrap and chill for 1 hour.
6. Grease a small 6-inch pie pan with cooking spray.
7. Place a skillet over high heat. Add oil. When the oil is heated, add onion and salt and sauté until it begins to become brown.
8. Add water and lower heat. Cook until onions turn golden brown. Turn off the heat.
9. Place a sheet of parchment paper over your countertop. Place the dough on the parchment paper.
10. Roll the dough with a rolling pin into a circle of about 8-9 inches.
11. Carefully invert the pie pan on the rolled dough in the center.
12. Invert again the entire thing along with the parchment paper (hold one hand below the parchment paper, underneath the rolled dough and one hand on the pie pan).
13. Carefully remove the paper and press the rolled dough on to the pie pan on the bottom as well as the sides. Crimp the excess rolled dough along the edges.

14. Spread the onions over the dough in the pan. Spread corn over it followed by tomatoes and jalapeños.
15. Sprinkle cheese on top.
16. Add eggs, whites, sour cream, milk, pepper, 1-tablespoon sour cream and salt into a bowl and whisk well.
17. Pour over the vegetables in the pie pan.
18. Bake in a preheated oven at 375° F for 30-40 minutes or set and firm in the center.
19. Remove from the oven and cool for 15 minutes.
20. Cut into 4 wedges and serve.

Black Beans Tacos

Serves: 3 (2 tacos each)

Nutritional values per serving:

Calories – 283, Fat – 9.3 g, Carbohydrate – 30 g, Protein - 20.4 g

Ingredients:

- 1 teaspoon olive oil
- ¼ teaspoons dried oregano
- 1 jalapeno pepper, seeded, minced
- ½ tablespoon low sodium soy sauce
- ½ package seitan (from an 8 ounce package, wheat gluten), finely chopped
- 6 taco shells
- 1 small onion, chopped
- 2 cloves garlic, minced
- ½ tablespoon dry sherry
- 7.5 ounces canned black beans, with its liquid
- ¼ teaspoon black pepper
- 1 cup shredded romaine lettuce
- Avocado salsa to serve

Method:

1. Place a nonstick skillet over medium heat. Add oil. When the oil is heated, add onion, garlic, jalapeño and oregano and sauté for 4-5 minutes.
2. Add dry sherry, soy sauce, beans, and seitan. Mix well. Cook until nearly dry.
3. Add pepper and stir.

4. Follow the directions on the package and make the taco shells.
5. Divide the filling among the taco shells. Top with lettuce and avocado salsa.

Chicken Fajitas

Serves: 2

Nutritional values per serving:

Calories – 210, Fat – 3 g, Carbohydrate – 29 g, Protein – 17 g

Ingredients:

- 4 ounces chicken breasts, skinless boneless, trimmed
- Salt to taste
- Freshly ground pepper to taste
- 1 tablespoon nonfat plain yogurt
- ½ tablespoon fresh cilantro, chopped
- A large pinch ground cumin
- 2 whole wheat flour tortillas
- 1 small tomato, thinly sliced

Method:

1. Place chicken in a glass bowl. Season with salt and pepper. Drizzle lime juice. Set aside for 10 minutes.
2. Add yogurt, cilantro, cumin, sour cream, salt and jalapeño into a bowl. Whisk well.
3. Grease a baking sheet with a little oil. Place chicken on the baking sheet.
4. Broil in a preheated oven for 3-4 minutes.
5. Add onion and stir. Broil for a few more minutes until the chicken is not pink anymore and cooked through.
6. Warm the tortillas following the instructions on the package.
7. Spread the tortillas on your countertop. Place chicken, lettuce leaves, onions and tomato slices.

8. Drizzle yogurt mixture on top. Roll and serve right away.

Mexican Grilled Cheese Sandwiches

Serves: 2

Nutritional values per serving:

Calories – 402, Fat – 22 g, Carbohydrate – 39 g, Protein – 11 g

Ingredients:

- 1 small sweet yellow pepper, chopped
- 1 teaspoon olive oil
- 1 tablespoon mayonnaise
- 6 tablespoons Mexican cheese blend, shredded
- 1 small green bell pepper, chopped
- 4 slices rye bread
- ½ cup fresh salsa, drained
- 1 tablespoon butter, softened

Method:

1. Place a skillet over medium heat. Add oil. When the oil is heated, add peppers and sauté until tender.
2. Apply mayonnaise on 2 slices of bread.
3. Divide the pepper mixture over it. Divide and spread salsa and cheese over the peppers.
4. Cover with the remaining 2 slices of bread.
5. Brush butter on the outside of the sandwiches.
6. Place a skillet over medium heat. Cook the sandwiches on both the sides until golden brown.
7. Cut into desired shape and serve.

Chapter Three: Dinner Recipes

Soups:

Tortilla Soup

Serves:

Nutritional values per serving:

Calories – 275, Fat – 12 g, Carbohydrate – 24 g, Protein – 19 g

Ingredients:

- 4 corn tortillas, halved cut into strips
- 1 ½ poblano peppers or Anaheim peppers, chopped
- 7 ounces canned diced tomatoes with green chilies along with the juices
- ¼ cup fresh cilantro, chopped
- ½ tablespoon canola oil
- 2 cups chicken broth
- ½ pound chicken thighs, trimmed cut into bite size pieces
- 1 teaspoon garlic, minced (optional)
- ¼ cup sharp cheddar cheese, shredded
- 1 small onion, chopped
- Salt to taste
- Pepper powder to taste
- ½ teaspoon ground cumin
- 1 tablespoon lime juice
- Cooking spray

Method:

1. Spread tortilla strips in a single layer on a large baking sheet. Spray cooking spray over it.
2. Bake in a preheated oven at 400° F for 12-15 minutes or until crisp.
3. Meanwhile, place a soup pot over medium heat. Add oil. When the oil is heated, add onions, poblano peppers and garlic and sauté until onions are translucent.
4. Add cumin and sauté for a few seconds.
5. Add broth, tomatoes and half the cilantro.
6. When it begins to boil, lower heat and cover with a lid. Cook until chicken is tender.
7. Turn off the heat and add lime juice, salt and pepper. Stir well.
8. Ladle into soup bowls. Divide the tortilla strips among the bowls. Garnish with cilantro and serve.

Vegan Taco Soup

Serves: 5

Nutritional values per serving:

Calories – 131, Fat – 7 g, Carbohydrate – 16 g, Protein – 2 g

Ingredients:

- 7.5 ounces canned kidney beans, with its liquid
- 7.5 ounces canned hominy, with its liquid
- 7.5 ounces canned pinto beans, with its liquid
- 7.5 ounces canned corn with its liquid
- 14 ounces canned diced tomatoes, with its liquid
- 4 ounces canned diced green chilies
- ½ cup salsa
- ¼ cup jalapeno, diced (optional)
- ½ package (from a 12 ounces package) vegan ground beef
- ½ package taco seasoning (from a 1 ¼ ounce package) or to taste
- ½ tablespoon garlic, minced
- 1 small onion, chopped
- 1 tablespoon oil

For garnish:

- A handful cilantro, chopped
- ¼ cup vegan sour cream
- 1 medium ripe avocado, peeled, pitted, chopped
- Tortilla chips as required

Method:

1. Place a soup pot over medium heat. Add all the beans, corn, tomatoes, green chilies, salsa and taco mix, jalapeños and salsa. Stir occasionally. Let it simmer for 10-12 minutes.
2. Place a skillet over medium heat. Add oil. When the oil is heated, add onions, garlic, vegan ground beef and sauté until cooked through. Transfer into the pot.
3. Place the pot over medium heat. Add rest of the ingredients of the soup into the pot and stir.
4. When it begins to boil, turn off the heat.
5. Ladle soup into soup bowls. Garnish with cilantro, avocado and cilantro. Finally, top with tortilla chips and serve.

Entrée's

Churrasco-Style Tofu Steaks with Hemp Chimichurri

Serves: 3

Nutritional values per serving: 2 tofu triangles with 1-tablespoon sauce

Calories – 278, Fat – 21 g, Carbohydrate – 8 g, Protein – 14 g

Ingredients:

- ½ cup fresh flat leaf parsley leaves
- 1 tablespoon hemp seeds
- 1 clove garlic
- ½ teaspoon salt, divided
- 1 package (14 ounces) extra firm block style tofu, drained, pressed of excess moisture
- ½ teaspoon onion powder
- ½ teaspoon ground cumin
- ½ tablespoon fresh lime juice
- Cooking spray
- ½ cup packed fresh cilantro leaves
- ½ tablespoon red wine vinegar
- Crushed red pepper to taste
- 2 ½ tablespoons extra-virgin olive oil
- 1 teaspoon garlic powder
- ½ teaspoon smoked paprika
- ¼ teaspoon pepper powder

Method:

1. To make sauce: Add cilantro, parsley, hemp seeds, lime juice, red pepper flakes, vinegar, garlic, salt and 2 tablespoons oil into a blender and blend until smooth.
2. Transfer into a bowl. Cover and set aside for a while for the flavors to set in.
3. Dry the tofu by patting with paper towels. Cut into 2 equal triangles. Cut each into 3 triangles. You are left with 6 triangles in all.
4. Place paper towels on a plate. Place the tofu triangles over it, in a single layer.
5. Add garlic powder, onion powder, cumin, paprika, salt and pepper into a small bowl and stir. Sprinkle this mixture over the tofu. Rub it well into the pieces.
6. Spray cooking spray over the tofu triangles.
7. Place a grill pan over medium high heat. Add ½ tablespoon oil. When the oil is heated, place tofu in the pan, do not overlap. Cook in batches if required.
8. Cook until the grill marks are prominent on the tofu and are well browned.
9. Remove the tofu from the pan and place on a baking sheet.
10. Bake in a preheated oven at 375° F for 5 minutes.
11. Place 2 tofu steaks on each plate. Drizzle 1-tablespoon sauce over the tofu on each plate and serve.

Grilled Chicken Thighs with Ancho-Tequila Glaze

Serves: 3

Nutritional values per serving: 2 chicken thighs with 2 teaspoons glaze and a lime wedge

Calories – 278, Fat – 10.8 g, Carbohydrate – 20.5 g, Protein – 21.7 g

Ingredients:

For chicken:

- ½ tablespoon ancho chili powder
- ¾ teaspoon granulated garlic
- ¾ teaspoon freshly ground pepper
- ¾ teaspoon sugar
- ¾ teaspoon ground cumin
- 6 bone-in chicken thighs (about 1 ¼ pounds)
- ½ teaspoon salt
- 2 teaspoons extra-virgin olive oil

For glaze:

- 3 tablespoons amber agave syrup
- 2 teaspoons hot sauce
- 2 teaspoons fresh lime juice
- Cooking spray
- 1 ½ tablespoons tequila
- 2 teaspoons butter
- Crushed red pepper to taste

To serve:

- 3 lime wedges
- A handful fresh cilantro, chopped (optional)

Method:

1. To make chicken: Add ancho chili powder, garlic, pepper, sugar, salt and cumin into a bowl and stir.
2. Dredge the chicken in it. Drizzle oil over it and toss well.
3. To make tequila glaze: Add agave syrup, hot sauce, lime juice, tequila, butter and red pepper into a bowl and add into a small saucepan. Turn off the heat.
4. Place the saucepan over medium heat. Simmer until it is reduced to 1/3 cup.
5. Preheat a grill. Spray the grill rack with cooking spray. Place chicken on the grill rack. Brush with 1-tablespoon tequila glaze. Grill for 15 minutes. Flip sides. Brush with 1-tablespoon tequila glaze. Grill for 15 minutes or until done.
6. Sprinkle cilantro on top. Serve 2 chicken thighs, 2 teaspoons glaze and a lime wedge in each serving.

Black Bean and Cheese Enchiladas with Ranchero Sauce

Serves: 3

Nutritional values per serving: 2 enchiladas and 1-tablespoon sour cream

Calories – 302, Fat – 12.9 g, Carbohydrate – 36.1 g, Protein – 17.3 g

Ingredients:

- 1 dried ancho chili, discard stem, deseeded
- 1 teaspoon olive oil
- 3 cloves garlic, sliced
- 1 cup vegetable broth
- 1 tablespoon tomato paste
- ½ tablespoon fresh lime juice
- 7.5 ounces canned black beans, rinsed, drained
- 2 green onions, thinly sliced, divided
- 1 cup water
- ½ cup yellow onion, chopped
- Salt to taste
- 1 tablespoon fresh oregano, chopped
- ¼ teaspoon ground cumin
- Red pepper powder to taste
- 1 cup low fat 4 cheese Mexican blend cheese, divided
- Cooking spray
- 3 tablespoons light sour cream
- 6 corn tortillas (6 inches each)

Method:

1. Add water and ancho chili into a saucepan. Place the saucepan over medium heat.
2. When it begins to boil, lower the heat and cook for 5 minutes. Turn off the heat and cool for a while.
3. Place a colander over a bowl. Drain the chilies in it. Retain the liquid.
4. Place a skillet over medium heat. Add oil. When the oil is heated, add onion and cook for a couple of minutes.
5. Add garlic and salt and sauté until brown. Stir occasionally.
6. Add broth, oregano, tomato paste and cumin. Simmer until thick.
7. Turn off the heat. Cool for a few minutes and transfer into a blender. Blend until smooth.
8. Transfer into a bowl. Add lime juice and red pepper and stir.
9. Add ½ cup cheese, beans and half the green onions into a bowl and stir.
10. Pour about 3-4 tablespoons sauce into a baking dish that is greased with cooking spray. Spread it all over the dish.
11. Place about 3 tablespoons of the bean mixture along the diameter of each of the tortillas.
12. Roll the tortillas and place with its seam side facing down in the baking dish, over the sauce layer.
13. Drizzle remaining sauce over the rolls. Top with remaining cheese.
14. Bake in a preheated oven at 400° F until the top is light brown.
15. Top with remaining green onions.

16. Place 2 enchiladas on each plate drizzled with 1-tablespoon sour cream.

Chicken Enchiladas

Serves: 3

Nutritional values per serving:

Calories – 262, Fat – 10.8, Carbohydrate – 22.8, Protein – 18.3

Ingredients:

- 2 cups cold water
- ½ tablespoon black peppercorns
- 1 chicken breast halves, skinless, boneless
- 1 medium carrot, peeled, cut into ½ inch pieces
- 1 jalapeño pepper, halved
- 5 ounces salsa Verde or enchilada sauce
- ½ cup tomatoes, chopped
- ¼ teaspoon kosher salt or to taste
- ¼ teaspoon ground red pepper or to taste
- 6 corn tortillas (6 inches each)
- 2 tablespoons sharp cheddar cheese, shredded
- 1 cup fat free chicken broth
- 3 cloves garlic, crushed
- ½ stalk celery, chopped
- 1 small onion, cut into wedges
- 2 tablespoons heavy whipping cream
- 2 tablespoons cilantro, chopped
- ¼ teaspoon ground cumin
- 2 ounce low fat cream cheese, softened
- Cooking spray

Method:

1. Place a soup pot over medium heat. Add water, broth, peppercorns, garlic, chicken, celery, carrot, jalapeno pepper, and onions.
2. When it begins to boil, lower heat and cover with a lid. Simmer until the chicken is cooked through.
3. Remove the chicken with a slotted spoon and place on your cutting board.
4. When cool enough to handle, shred the chicken with a pair of forks. Set aside.
5. Strain the solids remaining in the pot. Retain the liquid and discard the solids.
6. Pour the liquid back into the pot. Add salsa and stir.
7. Raise heat to medium high heat and cook until the liquid reduces to about ¾ cup. Lower heat to low heat and add cream. Turn off the heat.
8. Add chicken, tomato, cilantro, salt, cumin, cream cheese, and pepper into a bowl and stir.
9. Dip the tortillas in the sauce mixture to coat well. Place the chicken filling in the tortilla and roll the tortillas.
10. Place the rolled tortillas in a greased baking dish with the seam side facing down. Pour remaining sauce over the tortillas.
11. Sprinkle cheddar cheese.
12. Bake in a preheated oven at 400° F for about 20 minutes or until slightly brown.
13. Serve hot.

Fish Tacos in Lime Sauce

Serves: 5

Nutritional values per serving:

Calories – 167, Fat – 5.9 g, Carbohydrate – 16.1 g, Protein – 11.7 g

Ingredients:

- ½ package (from a 4.6 ounce package) taco shells
- ½ pound tilapia fillets
- ½ tablespoon olive oil
- 1 tablespoon taco seasoning mix
- 3 ounces plain yogurt
- ½ teaspoon white sugar
- Salt to taste
- 1 tablespoon fresh cilantro, chopped
- 1 small tomato, deseeded, chopped
- ½ teaspoon lime juice
- ¼ teaspoon lime zest, grated
- 2 cups coleslaw mix
- ½ small jalapeño chili, deseeded, finely chopped

Method:

1. Sprinkle taco seasoning over the fillets.
2. Place a skillet over medium heat. Add oil. When the oil is heated, place fish and cook for 3-4 minutes. Flip sides and cook for 3-4 minutes or until the fish flakes when pierced with a fork.
3. Turn off the heat. Remove fillets and place on your cutting board. When cool enough to handle, chop into bite size pieces.

4. Meanwhile, bake taco shells in a preheated oven at 325° F for about 5 minutes or until crisp.
5. Add yogurt, sugar, salt, lime juice and zest into a bowl and mix well.
6. Add coleslaw, jalapeño and cilantro and mix well.
7. Divide the fish and coleslaw among the taco shells. Divide the tomatoes and serve.

Chicken Verde Tacos

Serves: 2

Nutritional values per serving: 2 tacos

Calories – 210, Fat – 8.4 g, Carbohydrate – 10 g, Protein – 23 g

Ingredients:

- 1 cup shredded rotisserie chicken breast, skinless, boneless
- 4 corn tortillas (6 inches each)
- 2-3 tablespoons canola mayonnaise
- ¼ cup prepared salsa Verde
- 1 cup purple cabbage, thinly sliced

Method:

1. Place a saucepan over medium heat. Add chicken and salsa.
2. Heat thoroughly.
3. Follow the directions on the package and heat the tortillas.
4. Add cabbage and mayonnaise into a bowl. Mix well.
5. Spread the tortillas on a serving platter.
6. Divide and spread the chicken mixture on the tortillas. Divide the cabbage and spread over the chicken.
7. Roll and serve.

Grilled Skirt Steak and Roasted Tomatillo Sauce

Serves: 2

Nutritional values per serving:

Calories – 227, Fat – 11.4 g, Carbohydrate – 11 g, Protein – 19.9 g

Ingredients:

- ½ cup boiling water
- 1 ½ tablespoons fresh oregano, chopped, divided
- ½ tablespoon olive oil
- 4 cloves garlic, divided
- ¼ cup onions, sliced
- Cooking spray
- Freshly ground pepper to taste
- 1 tablespoon fresh cilantro, chopped
- 1 small guajillo chili, discard stem
- 1 tablespoon fresh lime juice, divided
- ½ pound skirt steak, trimmed
- 4 ounces tomatillos, husk removed
- Salt to taste
- A pinch sugar
- ¾ teaspoon ground cumin

Method:

1. Mince 2 cloves garlic. Crush 2 cloves garlic.
2. Place chili in a bowl. Pour boiling hot water over it. Let it soak for 10-15 minutes.
3. Discard the water and chop the chili into fine pieces.
4. Add chili, ½ tablespoon oregano, minced garlic, ¼ teaspoon cumin and ½ tablespoon lime juice into a

ziplock bag. Close the bag and shake until well combined.

5. Place steak in the bag and close the bag. Shake until well combined. Chill for an hour. Turn the bag a couple of times while it is chilling.
6. Place crushed garlic, onion and tomatillos on a rimmed baking sheet. Spray with cooking spray. Toss and spray again. Spread in a single layer.
7. Bake in a preheated oven at 450° F for about 20 minutes or until slightly brownish black on the skin.
8. Cool slightly and transfer into the blender. Add 1-tablespoon oregano, ¼ teaspoon cumin, salt, sugar and pepper into the blender and blend until smooth. Transfer into a bowl.
9. Remove the bag from the refrigerator and steak from the bag. Sprinkle salt and pepper all over the steak.
10. Place steak on a preheated grill (spray the grill rack with cooking spray before placing the steak) and grill for 2 minutes. Flip sides and grill for 2 minutes or when the internal temperature in the thickest part shows 135° F or according to the way you like it cooked.
11. When done, remove steak and place on your cutting board.
12. When cool enough to handle, slice steak diagonally into thin slices (across the grain).
13. Divide the steak into 2 serving plates. Spoon 3 tablespoons sauce on top. Garnish with cilantro and serve.

Mexican Corn Bread Casserole

Serves: 4

Nutritional values per serving:

Calories – 304, Fat – 16.3 g, Carbohydrate – 21.5 g, Protein – 18.2 g

Ingredients:

For meat base:

- ½ tablespoon olive oil
- ¼ red bell pepper, chopped
- ½ teaspoon minced garlic
- Cayenne pepper to taste
- ¼ cup frozen corn
- ½ cup salsa
- ½ small onion, chopped
- ½ pound ground beef
- ½ teaspoon chili powder
- Salt to taste
- Black pepper powder to taste
- ½ cup Mexican cheese blend, divided or use more to taste

For cornbread topping:

- ½ cup cornmeal
- ¼ teaspoon baking soda
- 1 egg, beaten
- Salt to taste
- ½ cup milk

Method:

1. Place a nonstick skillet over medium heat. Add oil. When the oil is heated, add onion and bell pepper and sauté until translucent.
2. Stir in beef, garlic, salt and spices. Mix well and cook until brown. Break it simultaneously as it cooks.
3. Add corn and mix well. Discard excess fat from the pan.
4. Add 2 tablespoons cheese and stir. Transfer into a casserole dish.
5. Spread salsa over the beef layer.
6. To make cornmeal bread topping: Add cornmeal, baking soda and salt into a bowl and stir.
7. Stir in the egg and milk until well combined.
8. Spread the cornmeal mixture over the salsa layer. Sprinkle remaining cheese.
9. Bake in a preheated oven at 425° F for about 20 – 30 minutes or until top is brown.
10. Remove from the oven and serve after 10 minutes.

Cochinita Pibil (Mexican Pulled Pork in Annatto Sauce)

Serves: 6

Nutritional values per serving:

Calories – 422, Fat – 25.6 g, Carbohydrate – 8.3 g, Protein – 37.6 g

Ingredients:

For marinade:

- 1.5 ounces achiote paste
- 1 clove garlic
- ¼ cup lemon juice
- 1 cup orange juice
- 2 tablespoons white vinegar
- ½ tablespoon black pepper powder
- 2.5 pounds pork roast shoulder
- ½ tablespoon lard
- 1 small onion, chopped
- 1 tablespoon salt
- ½ tablespoon dried Mexican oregano
- Salt to taste
- Pepper to taste

For habanero sauce:

- 1 small red onion, chopped
- 2 tablespoons lemon juice
- ½ cup lukewarm water
- ½ teaspoon dried oregano
- 1-2 habanero chilies, deseeded, sliced

- 2 tablespoons white vinegar
- Salt to taste
- Black pepper powder to taste

Method:

1. To marinade: Add achiote paste, onion, garlic, vinegar, lemon juice, orange juice, 1 tablespoon salt, ½ tablespoon Mexican oregano and ½ tablespoon black pepper into a blender and blend until smooth.
2. Sprinkle salt and pepper over the pork and rub it well into it. Place meat in a Dutch oven.
3. Add lard and blended marinade over it. Cover with lid.
4. Place pot over medium heat. When it begins to boil, lower heat and cook until meat is tender. This may take a couple of hours.
5. When done, remove meat and place on your cutting board. When cool enough to handle, shred with a pair of forks and add it back into the pot. Alternately, you can cook in an instant pot or pressure cooker if you own one. It will be much faster.
6. Simmer for some more time until the liquid in the pot has reduced considerably.
7. Meanwhile to make habanero sauce: Add all the ingredients of habanero sauce into a bowl and mix well. Cover and set aside for a while for the flavors to set in.
8. Serve meat with habanero sauce.

Traditional Chilaquiles

Serves: 4

Nutritional values per serving:

Calories – 297, Fat – 13.2 g, Carbohydrate – 22.3 g, Protein – 22.6 g

Ingredients:

- 4 fresh tomatillos, husk removed
- 1 small poblano pepper, peeled, deseeded, chopped
- 1 small bunch cilantro, chopped
- 1 small onion, coarsely chopped
- 1 small jalapeño, deseeded, chopped
- 2 cloves garlic, peeled
- 1 ½ cups cooked chicken
- 6 white corn tortillas (6 inches each), cut into 3 inch strips
- 6 tablespoons Monterey Jack cheese, shredded
- 2-3 fresh mint leaves
- 2 tablespoons vegetable oil
- Salt to taste
- 6 tablespoons Pepper Jack cheese

Method:

1. Add tomatillos, poblano pepper, onion, jalapeño pepper, garlic, cilantro, salt and mint into a blender and blend until smooth.
2. Pour into a saucepan. Place saucepan over medium low heat.
3. Simmer until thick. Stir frequently. Stir in the chicken and cook until chicken is thoroughly heated.

4. Place a skillet over medium heat. Add oil. When the oil is heated, add tortilla strips and cook until brown. Cook in batches. Remove with a slotted spoon and place on a plate lined with paper towels.
5. Spread half the fried tortillas in a baking dish. Layer with half the tomatillo sauce.
6. Add both the cheeses in a bowl and stir. Sprinkle half the cheese mixture over the sauce.
7. Repeat the above 2 steps once more.
8. Bake in a preheated oven at 425° F for about 20 – 30 minutes or until top is brown and bubbling
9. Cool for 5 minutes and serve.

Crab Quesadillas

Serves: 2

Nutritional values per serving:

Calories – 302, Fat – 10 g, Carbohydrate – 29 g, Protein – 24 g

Ingredients:

- ½ cup low fat cheddar cheese, shredded
- 2 scallions, chopped
- ¼ cup fresh cilantro, chopped
- ½ teaspoon orange zest, freshly grated
- 4 ounces pasteurized crabmeat, drain if necessary
- 1 teaspoon canola oil, divided
- 1 ounce low fat cream cheese, softened
- 1 small red bell pepper, finely chopped
- 1 tablespoon pickled jalapeños, chopped (optional)
- 2 teaspoons orange juice
- 2 whole wheat tortillas (8 inches each)

Method:

1. Place tortillas on your countertop.
2. Add rest of the ingredients except crab and oil into a bowl and mix until well combined.
3. Add crab and fold gently. Divide and spread the mixture on one half of the tortillas.
4. Fold the other half of the tortilla over the filling.
5. Place a large nonstick skillet over medium heat. Add oil. When the oil is heated, place the quesadillas and cook until golden brown. Flip sides and cook the other side until golden brown.
6. Cut into wedges if desired and serve.

Mexican Bean Burgers with Lime Yogurt & Salsa

Serves: 3

Nutritional values per serving:

Calories – 195, Fat – 3 g, Carbohydrate – 33 g, Protein – 11 g

Ingredients:

- 1 can (14 ounces) kidney beans, rinsed, drained
- ¼ cup fresh cilantro, finely chopped
- 3.5 ounces fresh salsa
- 1 teaspoon lime juice
- 1.75 ounces breadcrumbs
- 1 teaspoon mild chili powder
- 1 small egg
- 2.5 ounces low fat plain yogurt
- 3 whole meal burger buns, split
- Avocado slices to serve
- 3 lettuce leaves
- 3 slices red onion
- Salt to taste
- Pepper to taste

Method:

1. Add beans into a bowl and mash with a potato masher.
2. Stir in the breadcrumbs, half the cilantro, chili powder, 1-tablespoon salsa, salt and pepper. Mix well. Divide the mixture into 3 equal portions.
3. Moisten your hands and shape into burgers and place on a nonstick baking sheet.

4. Grill on a preheated grill until golden brown on both the sides. It should take 4-5 minutes per side.
5. Meanwhile, add yogurt, lime, salt, pepper and remaining cilantro leaves into a bowl and stir.
6. Spread a little of the yogurt mixture on the cut half of the buns.
7. Place a lettuce leaf on the bottom half over the buns. Layer with avocado slices followed by an onion slice and a burger.
8. Spread a little yogurt mixture and finally salsa. Cover with the top halves of the bun.
9. Serve.

Side Dishes

Mexican Crispy Roasted Potatoes

Serves: 2

Nutritional values per serving:

Calories – 256, Fat – 12 g, Carbohydrate – 29 g, Protein – 5 g

Ingredients:

- ¾ pound petite red potatoes, rinsed, quartered
- ¾ teaspoon slat
- ¼ teaspoon dried oregano
- 1/8 teaspoon garlic powder
- ¼ cup parmesan cheese, freshly grated
- 1 tablespoon olive oil
- ¼ teaspoon ancho chili powder
- 1/8 teaspoon coriander powder
- Black pepper powder to taste
- Cayenne pepper to taste
- A handful fresh cilantro, finely chopped

Method:

1. Place a sheet of parchment paper on a baking sheet. Spray cooking spray over it.
2. Add all the spices, oregano, salt and oil into a bowl and mix well. Add potatoes and stir until the potatoes are well coated with the spice mixture.
3. Spread the potatoes on the prepared baking sheet. Spread in a single layer.

4. Bake in a preheated oven at 400° F for about 20 – 30 minutes. Flip sides a couple of times while baking. Bake until crisp.
5. Garnish with cilantro and serve.

Mexican Rice

Serves: 2

Nutritional values per serving:

Calories – 291, Fat – 11 g, Carbohydrate – 42.4 g, Protein – 4.8 g

Ingredients:

- 1 ½ tablespoons vegetable oil
- ½ teaspoon garlic salt
- 1 small onion, chopped
- ½ cup long grain rice, rinsed
- ¼ teaspoon ground cumin
- 1 cup chicken broth
- ¼ cup tomato sauce

Method:

1. Place a saucepan over medium heat. Add oil. When the oil is heated, add rice, cumin and salt and sauté until golden in color.
2. Add onions and sauté until onions are translucent. Add tomato sauce and broth.
3. When it begins to boil, cover with a lid and cook until dry and the rice is cooked.
4. Turn off the heat. Let it rest for 5-10 minutes.
5. Fluff the rice with a fork gently and serve.

Pinto Beans with Mexican-Style Seasonings

Serves: 4

Nutritional values per serving:

Calories – 267, Fat – 5.2 g, Carbohydrate – 40.9 g, Protein – 16.4 g

Ingredients:

- ½ pound dried pinto beans, rinsed
- ¼ pound bacon, cut into ½ inch pieces
- ½ tablespoon chili powder or to taste
- ¾ teaspoon garlic powder
- Salt to taste
- 1 can (10 ounces) diced tomatoes with green chilies
- 1 small yellow onion, chopped
- ½ tablespoon ground cumin or to taste
- ¼ cup fresh cilantro, chopped

Method:

1. Add pinto beans into a pot. Cover with water (at least 2-3 inches above the beans). Soak for 7-8 hours.
2. Drain and add enough fresh water to cover the beans. Add rest of the ingredients except salt and cilantro.
3. When it begins to boil, lower heat and cover with a lid. Simmer until tender. It may take 2-3 hours. Alternately, you can cook in an instant pot or pressure cooker if you own one. It will be much faster.
4. Add salt and cilantro and cook until very soft. This can take 40-50 minutes.

Rajas Con Crema, Elote Y, Queso (Creamy Poblano Peppers and Sweet Corn)

Serves: 2

Nutritional values per serving:

Calories – 347, Fat – 29.1 g, Carbohydrate – 13 g, Protein – 9.2 g

Ingredients:

- 2 poblano peppers
- 1 small ear corn, kernels removed
- 1 tablespoon vegetable oil, divided
- 1 cup water
- ½ tablespoon butter
- 1 teaspoon chicken bouillon granules
- 2 ¼ ounces Mexican Manchego cheese, grated
- ¼ cup heavy whipping cream

Method:

1. Place a sheet of foil on a baking sheet. Brush poblano peppers with ½ tablespoon oil and place over the baking sheet.
2. Bake in a preheated oven at 500° F for about 20 – 30 minutes. Flip sides halfway through baking.
3. Remove the peppers and place in a bowl. Cover the bowl with cling wrap. Let it rest for 15 minutes. Discard the skin, stem and seeds of the peppers and cut into strips.
4. Cook the corn kernels in a pot of boiling water until tender. Drain and set aside.
5. Place a saucepan over medium heat. Add ½ tablespoon vegetable oil and butter. When butter

melts, add onions and sauté until translucent. Stir in corn, chicken bouillon granules and poblano pepper and sauté for 2-3 minutes.

6. Lower heat and add Manchego cheese and cream. Mix well. Simmer for a few minutes until the cheese is melted.

Chapter Four: Traditional Mexican Salsa Recipes

Authentic Mexican Salsa

Serves: 8

Nutritional values per serving: 1 ounce

Calories – 9.7, Fat – 0.1 g, Carbohydrate – 2.2 g, Protein – 0.3 g

Ingredients:

- 6-7 dried arbol chili (Use lesser for a milder salsa), discard stems
- ¼ small onion, chopped
- ½ bunch cilantro, chopped
- ½ teaspoon lemon juice or ½ teaspoon lime juice
- Salt to taste
- 7 ounces canned stewed tomatoes with its juice
- ½ jalapeno, chopped
- 1 clove garlic, peeled
- Pepper powder to taste

Method:

1. Add all the ingredients into a blender and blend until the consistency you desire is achieved.
2. Transfer into a bowl. Cover and set aside for a while in the refrigerator, for the flavors to set in.

Mexican Salsa

Serves: 6-7

Nutritional values per serving: ¼ cup

Calories –23, Fat – 0 g, Carbohydrate – 5 g, Protein – 1 g

Ingredients:

- 1-2 jalapeño peppers
- 1 small clove garlic, halved
- 1 small onion, quartered
- 2 springs cilantro
- 1 ½ cans (14.5 ounces each) whole tomatoes, drained
- Salt to taste

Method:

1. Take a fork and prick the jalapeño at several places.
2. Place a nonstick skillet over medium heat. When the pan is heated, place the jalapeño. Sauté until charred. Stir occasionally.
3. Transfer the peppers into a bowl. Cover and set aside for a while. Discard the skin, stem and seeds.
4. Add onion and garlic into a blender and pulse for about 10-15 seconds.
5. Add rest of the ingredients and pulse until the consistency you desire is achieved.
6. Transfer into a bowl. Cover and set aside for a while in the refrigerator, for the flavors to set in.

Pico de Gallo

Serves: 8

Nutritional values per serving:

Calories – 10, Fat – 0.1 g, Carbohydrate – 2.2 g, Protein – 0.4 g

Ingredients:

- 4 medium tomatoes, finely chopped
- 1 cup red onion, minced
- 2 Serrano peppers or jalapeño peppers, deseeded, minced
- ¼ cup fresh cilantro, minced
- 3 tablespoons lime juice
- 1/8 teaspoon ground cumin
- 1/8 teaspoon garlic powder
- 1 clove garlic, peeled, minced
- ½ teaspoon sea salt or to taste
- Pepper powder to taste

Method:

1. Mix together all the ingredients in a bowl.
2. Taste and add more seasonings if required.
3. Cover and set aside for a while in the refrigerator, for the flavors to set in.

Authentic Mole

Serves: 12

Nutritional values per serving: ½ cup

Calories – 170, Fat – 11.7 g, Carbohydrate – 16.4 g, Protein – 2 g

Ingredients:

- 2-3 new Mexican chilies, remove stems, deseeded
- 1-2 chipotle chilies, remove stems, deseeded
- 1 guajillo chili, remove stem, deseeded
- 2 ancho chilies, remove stems, deseeded, retain the seeds
- 1 tablespoon peanuts, hulled, unsalted
- 1 tablespoon sesame seeds
- 1 small onion, chopped into chunks
- 1 tablespoon almonds, sliced
- ½ teaspoon peppercorns
- ½ pound Roma tomatoes, halved
- ½ tortilla
- ¼ tablet Mexican chocolate
- 2-3 cloves garlic, smashed
- 1 stick cinnamon
- 1 tablespoon low sodium chicken stock
- ½ cup sugar
- ½ slice wheat bread
- ½ ounce raisins
- ½ cup grape seed oil or 1 ¾ cup olive oil
- 1 teaspoon salt or to taste
- 1 quart water

Method:

1. Add water into a pot and place it over medium heat for boiling.
2. Meanwhile, add ancho chili seeds, sesame seeds, peanuts, almonds, and peppercorns into a small saucepan and roast it over medium heat. When it is lightly toasted, turn off the heat. Let it cool.
3. Place the chilies in a grill pan and toast over medium heat. Add it to the boiling water.
4. Add onion and garlic to the same pan and sauté for a few minutes until toasted. Transfer into the boiling water.
5. In the same grill pan toast tomatoes, cinnamon, and raisins. Transfer into the boiling water. Add the roasted seeds, grape seed oil, chocolate, tortilla, chicken stock, bread, and salt. Lower heat and simmer for 30 minutes.
6. Blend the entire ingredients of the pot using an immersion blender.
7. Add sugar and simmer uncovered until the sauce thickens.

Salsa Roja

Serves: 16

Nutritional values per serving:

Calories – 24, Fat – 2 g, Carbohydrate – 5 g, Protein – 1 g

Ingredients:

- 10 plum (Roma) tomatoes, halved
- 24 stalks cilantro
- 4 tablespoons cooking oil
- 2 white onions, quartered
- 4 cloves garlic, peeled
- 8 cups water
- 4 Serrano chilies, discard stems
- Salt to taste

Method:

1. Set aside the cilantro and oil and add rest of the ingredients into a pot.
2. Place the pot over medium heat. When it begins to boil, lower the heat and cook for 20 minutes. Turn off the heat. Cool for a while.
3. Transfer into a blender. Add cilantro and blend until smooth.
4. Place the pot over medium heat. When the pot is dry, add oil. When the oil is heated, add the blended mixture.
5. Lower the heat and let it cook for 20-30 minutes.
6. Taste and adjust the salt if necessary.
7. Use as required. Leftovers can be added to freezer safe containers or bags and frozen until use.

Salsa Verde Cruda

Makes: 4 cups

Nutritional values per serving: ¼ cup

Calories – 48, Fat – 3 g, Carbohydrate – 5 g, Protein – 1 g

Ingredients:

- 2 pounds tomatillos, husked, rinsed, chopped
- ¼ cup white onion, chopped
- ½ cup cilantro, chopped
- 2 large cloves garlic, peeled
- 2 fresh Serrano chilies or jalapeño chilies, chopped
- 1 teaspoon kosher salt or coarse sea salt
- 2 ripe avocadoes, peeled, pitted, chopped

Method:

1. Add all the ingredients into a blender and blend until smooth.
2. Taste and add more salt if required.
3. Transfer into a bowl. Refrigerate until use.

Guacamole

Serves: 4

Nutritional values per serving:

Calories – 93, Fat – 8 g, Carbohydrate – 6 g, Protein – 1 g

Ingredients:

- 7.5 ounces, peeled, seeded, mashed with a fork
- 1 small clove garlic, finely diced or grated
- 2 tablespoons lime juice or to taste
- 3 tablespoons finely chopped red onion
- 1 teaspoon sea salt
- ¼ cup fresh cilantro, finely chopped
- 1 jalapeno pepper, finely sliced (optional)
- Freshly ground black pepper to taste

Method:

1. Mix together all the ingredients in a bowl.
2. Taste and add more salt if required.
3. Transfer to a bowl. Refrigerate until use.

Chapter Five: Mexican Appetizer Recipes

Antojitos Minis

Serves: 12

Nutritional values per serving:

Calories – 109, Fat – 5 g, Carbohydrate – 11.4 g, Protein – 4.6 g

Ingredients:

- 2 flour tortillas (12 inches each)
- 1.5 ounces Monterey Jack cheese, shredded
- 1.5 ounces white cheddar cheese, shredded
- 1.5 ounces cheddar cheese
- ½ cup red bell pepper, chopped
- 3 tablespoons canned black beans, drained
- Chili powder to taste
- 1 small tomato, diced
- 1 green onion, chopped
- 1 tablespoon salsa

Method:

1. Grease a 12-count muffin pan with cooking spray. Place the tortillas on your countertop. Using a cookie cutter, make 6 rounds of each tortilla.
2. Place a round of tortilla in each of the muffin cups.
3. Add rest of the ingredients into the muffin cups in whatever order you desire.
4. Bake in a preheated oven at 420° F until the cheese is melted and light brown.
5. Carefully remove from the muffin cups.
6. Serve.

Corn Tortilla Chips

Serves: 24

Nutritional values per serving:

Calories – 126, Fat – 8.1 g, Carbohydrate – 12.5 g, Protein – 1.6 g

Ingredients:

- 2 packages corn tortillas (12 ounces each), cut each into 6 wedges
- Oil to fry, as required
- Salt to taste

Method:

1. Place a small deep pan over medium heat. Add oil up to half. Let the oil heat.
2. When the oil is heated to 375° F fry the tortilla pieces in batches until crisp.
3. Remove with a slotted spoon and place over plates lined with paper towels.
4. Sprinkle salt after 3-4 minutes.
5. Serve.
6. Store leftovers in airtight containers.

Spicy Tortilla Roll-Ups

Serves: 15

Nutritional values per serving:

Calories – 109, Fat – 2.8 g, Carbohydrate – 14.2 g, Protein – 2.8 g

Ingredients:

- 4 ounces cream cheese, softened
- 2 ounces canned diced green chilies
- 1 green onion, minced
- A handful fresh cilantro, chopped
- 1 ounce canned black olives, chopped
- 2 ounces jarred sliced pimento peppers, drained
- 1.5 tablespoons hot pepper sauce
- 5 flour tortillas (10 inches each)

Method:

1. Spread the tortillas on your countertop.
2. Add rest of the ingredients into a bowl and mix until well combined.
3. Spread over the tortillas. Roll and place on a tray with the seam side facing down.
4. Slice and serve.

Crispy Tofu Nachos

Serves: 4

Nutritional values per serving:

Calories – 330, Fat – 14 g, Carbohydrate – 23 g, Protein – 18 g

Ingredients:

For tofu:

- ½ package (from a 15 ounces package) extra firm tofu, drained, press out the excess liquid, chop into 1 inch cubes
- ¼ packet taco seasoning or to taste
- ½ tablespoon olive oil

For nachos:

- ½ bag tortilla chips
- 1 ounce canned mild green chilies
- ½ cup part skim mozzarella cheese
- 2/3 cup part skim cheddar cheese, grated
- 1 habanero chili, deseeded, chopped
- 1 jalapeño chili, deseeded, chopped
- 7 ounces canned diced tomatoes, drained
- 1 small avocado, peeled, pitted, chopped
- A handful fresh cilantro, chopped, to garnish

Method:

1. Place tofu in a bowl. Sprinkle taco seasoning over it. Toss well. Drizzle oil and toss well.
2. Transfer onto a baking sheet that is greased with baking spray. Spread it in a single layer.

3. Bake in a preheated oven at 425° F for 10 minutes. Flip sides a couple of times. Bake until crisp.
4. Meanwhile, place half the tortilla chips in a large baking dish that is greased with cooking spray. Place some of the tofu over the chips.
5. Mix together both the cheeses in a bowl. Sprinkle ½ cup cheese and a little jalapeño.
6. Place another layer of chips. Layer with some more tofu, tomatoes and a little more cheese.
7. Sprinkle remaining jalapeños, habanero chili, canned green chili and remaining cheese.
8. Bake in a preheated oven at 425° F for about 15-20 minutes.
9. Sprinkle avocado and cilantro on top.
10. Divide into 4 equal portions and serve immediately.

Mexican Egg Rolls

Serves: 7

Nutritional values per serving:

Calories – 286, Fat – 17.2 g, Carbohydrate – 19 g, Protein – 12.5 g

Ingredients:

- ½ package (from a 14 ounces package) egg roll wrappers
- ½ package (from a 1.25 ounce package) taco seasoning mix
- 1 cup pepper Jack cheese, shredded
- ½ pound lean ground beef
- 2 ounces canned diced chilies, drained
- Oil to fry, as required

Method:

1. Place a skillet over medium high heat. Add beef. Sauté until brown. Break it simultaneously as it cooks. Add taco seasoning and stir. Drain excess fat remaining in the pan. Turn off the heat and let it cool for a while.
2. Place a small deep pan over medium heat. Add oil up to half. Let the oil heat.
3. Place an egg roll wrapper on your countertop. Place a heaped tablespoon of beef mixture in the center of the wrapper. Place a little green chilies and cheese.
4. Roll the wrapper following the instructions of the package. Moisten the edges with water if desired to seal firmly.
5. Repeat the above step with the remaining wrappers.

6. When the oil is heated to 375° F fry the egg rolls in batches until golden brown all over.
7. Remove with a slotted spoon and place over a plate lined with paper towels.
8. Serve immediately.

Mini Tostadas

Serves: 20

Nutritional values per serving: 1 round

Calories – 50, Fat – 3 g, Carbohydrate – 4 g, Protein – 2 g

Ingredients:

- 4 flour tortillas
- 8 ounces Old El Paso refried beans
- 4 ounces Mexican cheese blend, finely shredded
- Cooking spray
- ¼ cup green onion, sliced
- 1/3 cup sour cream

Method:

1. The rack in the oven must be placed in the lower most position.
2. Place the tortillas on your countertop. Spray with cooking spray. Using a cookie cutter (2 ½ inches), make 5 rounds from each tortilla and place on a baking sheet, the sprayed side facing down.
3. Spread refried beans over the tortilla rounds. Sprinkle most of the onions over the beans. Sprinkle cheese over the onions.
4. Bake in a preheated oven at 400° F for about 15-20 minutes. The tortillas should be crisp.
5. Drizzle about a teaspoon of sour cream on each round. Sprinkle remaining onions on top and serve right away.

Jalapeño Chicken Wraps

Serves: 7-8

Nutritional values per serving: 2

Calories – 101, Fat – 6 g, Carbohydrate – 2 g, Protein – 10 g

Ingredients:

- ½ pound chicken breasts, skinless, boneless, cut into 2 x 2 ½ inch strips
- ½ tablespoon onion powder
- ½ tablespoon garlic powder
- ½ tablespoon pepper powder
- ½ teaspoon paprika
- ½ tablespoon onion powder
- 1 teaspoon seasoned salt
- 1 small onions, cut into strips
- ½ pound sliced bacon, halved widthwise
- 7-8 jalapeño peppers, halved, deseeded
- Blue cheese salad dressing to serve

Method:

1. Add all the spices and seasoned salt into a ziplock bag. Shake to mix the spices.
2. Add chicken and shake again until the chicken is coated.
3. Place one chicken strip and one onion strip in each of the jalapeño halves.
4. Wrap the filled jalapeño halves with bacon strips. Fasten with toothpicks.
5. Grill on a preheated grill until the chicken is cooked and bacon is crisp on the outside.
6. Serve with blue cheese dressing.

Chapter Six: Desserts

Caramel Crème Brulée

Serves: 7

Nutritional values per serving: ½ cup

Calories – 452, Fat – 35 g, Carbohydrate – 28 g, Protein – 6 g

Ingredients:

- 2 ¼ cups heavy whipping cream
- 8 egg yolks
- 1 ½ teaspoons caramel extract
- 3 tablespoons packed brown sugar
- ¾ cup half and half
- ½ cup + 3 tablespoons sugar, divided
- 1/8 teaspoon salt

Method:

1. Place a saucepan over medium heat. Add whipping cream and half and half and stir. Turn off the heat when bubbles are formed around the edges of the pan.
2. Add yolks, ½ cup sugar, salt and caramel extract. Whisk until well combined. It should not be frothy.
3. Add the warmed cream slowly and stir gently.
4. Transfer the mixture into a baking dish. Place the baking dish in a large baking pan. There should be enough space between the baking dish and the baking pan from all the sides.
5. Place pan in the oven. Pour enough hot water into the baking pan carefully. It should be at least an inch in height from the bottom of the baking dish.

6. Bake in a preheated oven at 325° F for about 40-50 minutes or until set in the center.
7. Remove the baking dish from the oven and place on a wire rack. Let it cool completely.
8. Chill until use.
9. To use: Mix together in a bowl, the remaining sugar and brown sugar and sprinkle over the custard.
10. Broil in a preheated broiler for a few minutes until the sugar is golden brown.
11. Serve right away or warm.

Strawberry-Mango Margarita Compote

Serves: 8

Nutritional values per serving:

Calories – 130, Fat – 1 g, Carbohydrate – 26 g, Protein – 1 g

Ingredients:

- 4 cups strawberries, hulled, halved or quartered depending on the size
- ¼ cup sugar + extra to dip
- ¼ cup lime juice + extra for the glasses
- 3 tablespoons Triple Sec or other orange liqueur
- 4 cups mango, chopped (about 2 large mangoes)
- 2 teaspoons lime zest, freshly grated
- 3 tablespoons tequila

Method:

1. Add strawberries, sugar, lime juice Triple sec, mango, lime zest and tequila into a bowl. Toss well. Cover and set aside for the flavors to set in. chill for 3-4 hours if desired.
2. Brush the rims of 8 margarita glasses with lime juice. Dredge in sugar.
3. Carefully add the strawberry mixture with a spoon and serve.

Mexican Chocolate Meringues

Serves: 24

Nutritional values per serving:

Calories – 32, Fat – 1 g, Carbohydrate – 6 g, Protein – 1 g

Ingredients:

- ¼ cup almonds, slivered
- 2 ½ tablespoons Dutch process cocoa powder
- ¾ teaspoon ground cinnamon
- 1/8 teaspoon cream of tartar
- 1/8 teaspoon almond extract
- 1/8 teaspoon vanilla extract
- ½ cup sugar, divided
- 1 ½ tablespoons cornstarch
- 2 large egg whites
- ¾ ounce semi –sweet or bittersweet chocolate

Method:

1. Place almonds on a baking sheet. Spread it evenly.
2. Bake in a preheated oven at 350° F for about 4-5 minutes.
3. Remove the almonds from the oven and cool completely.
4. Place a sheet of parchment paper on a large baking sheet.
5. Add almonds and about 3 tablespoons sugar into the food processor bowl. Pulse until finely chopped.
6. Add cornstarch, cocoa, cornstarch and cinnamon and pulse until well combined.
7. Add egg whites into a mixing bowl. Set the electric mixer on low speed and beat until foamy.

8. Set the mixer on medium speed and beat in the cream of tartar. Beat until soft peaks are formed.
9. Add remaining sugar, a little at a time and beat each time. Beat until moist and firm peaks are formed.
10. Add vanilla extract and almond extract and beat until well combined.
11. Add almond mixture and fold gently.
12. Drop small mounds of the batter (a heaped teaspoon of the batter in each mound) on the prepared baking sheet. Leave a gap of about an inch between the mounds.
13. Bake in a preheated oven at 350° F for about 60 -70 minutes or until set in the center.
14. When done, let it remain in the oven for an hour.
15. Remove the meringues from the parchment paper.
16. Melt the chocolate either in a double boiler or in a microwave. Brush thinly, the meringues with melted chocolate, on the flat side.
17. Place with the chocolate side facing up on the baking sheet.
18. Serve when the chocolate is firm.

Original Mexican Flan Napolitano

Serves: 6

Nutritional values per serving:

Calories – 261, Fat – 13.9 g, Carbohydrate – 26 g, Protein – 8.9 g

Ingredients:

- 2 tablespoons white sugar
- 7 ounces canned evaporated milk
- 4 ounces cream cheese, softened
- 7 ounces canned sweetened condensed milk
- 3 medium eggs
- ½ teaspoon vanilla extract

Method:

1. For the topping: Place a heavy bottomed pan over medium heat. Add sugar. Cook until the sugar turns golden brown. Do not stir.
2. Pour into an ungreased baking dish. Swirl the dish to coat the bottom of the dish well.
3. Add rest of the ingredients into a blender and blend until smooth. Pour this mixture over the caramelized layer in the baking dish.
4. Place the baking in a larger glass baking dish. Fill the larger baking dish with water covering about an inch. Place the baking dish in the center of the oven rack.
5. Bake in a preheated oven at 350 ° F about an hour or until set.
6. Remove the baking dish from water and keep aside to cool.
7. Refrigerate overnight.

8. To serve: Run a knife around the edges and invert on to a large rimmed plate. Slice into wedges. Pour the remaining liquid in the dish over the wedges and serve.

Mexican Fried Ice Cream Dessert

Serves: 7

Nutritional values per serving:

Calories – 210, Fat – 10 g, Carbohydrate – 26 g, Protein – 2 g

Ingredients:

- 1 tablespoon butter
- ½ cup crushed Cinnamon Toast Crunch cereal (about 1 cup before crushing)
- ¼ cup packed brown sugar
- ½ teaspoon ground cinnamon
- ¼ cup sliced almonds
- ¼ cup shredded coconut
- ¾ quart vanilla ice cream

Method:

1. Place a skillet over medium heat. Add butter. When butter melts, add almonds and sauté for 2-3 minutes. Turn off the heat.
2. Add coconut crushed cereal and brown sugar and stir. Transfer into the bottom of a baking dish. Do not grease the baking dish. Press it on to the bottom of the dish.
3. Bake in a preheated oven at 375 ° F for 5 minutes. Freeze for 30 minutes.
4. Place ice cream in a bowl. When it softens slightly, add cinnamon and stir.
5. Spread over the crust evenly. Cover the dish with cling wrap and place in the freezer for 6-8 hours until well set.
6. Cut into equal pieces and serve.

Churros

Serves: 3

Nutritional values per serving:

Calories – 691, Fat – 51.1 g, Carbohydrate – 57.1 g, Protein – 3.1 g

Ingredients:

For churros:

- ½ cup all- purpose flour
- ½ cup water
- 1 tablespoon vegetable oil
- 6 teaspoons granulated sugar
- ¼ teaspoon salt
- 2 cups vegetable oil for frying

For cinnamon sugar:

- 1 teaspoon ground cinnamon
- ¼ cup granulated sugar

Method:

1. To make cinnamon sugar: Add ground cinnamon and sugar into a bowl and stir. Set aside.
2. To make churros: Place a small saucepan over medium heat. Add 1 tablespoon vegetable oil, 1 tablespoon granulated sugar, and salt and stir.
3. When it begins to boil, turn off the heat and add flour. Whisk until a smooth dough is formed.
4. Place the dough in a canvas pastry bag, which has a nozzle.

5. Take a small deep pan and add about 2 cups vegetable oil into it. Place the pan over medium heat and let the oil heat.
6. When the oil reaches 375° F, pipe the dough from the pastry bag. The churros should be about 4 inches long. As it reaches 4 inches, cut with a knife.
7. Similarly, make the remaining churros. Fry the churros in batches.
8. Fry until golden brown. Remove and place on a plate lined with paper towels.
9. Dredge the churros in the cinnamon sugar mixture and serve.

Broiled Mango

Serves: 4

Nutritional values per serving:

Calories – 102, Fat – 1 g, Carbohydrate – 26 g, Protein – 1 g

Ingredients:

- Lime juice, as required
- 2 mangoes, peeled, deseeded, sliced

Method:

1. Place rack in the upper third position in the oven. Preheat the oven.
2. Place a sheet of foil in a broiler pan.
3. Place mangoes in a single layer in the pan.
4. Broil for 8-10 minutes or brown spots appear at different places on the mango slices.
5. Sprinkle lime juice on top and serve.

Pastel de Tres Leches (Three Milk Cake)

Serves: 6

Nutritional values per serving:

Calories – 396, Fat – 18.8 g, Carbohydrate – 48.2 g, Protein – 9.8 g

Ingredients:

- 3 eggs, separated
- ½ cup all-purpose flour
- ¼ cup milk
- ½ cup heavy whipping cream
- 6 ounces canned evaporated milk
- ½ cup fresh strawberries, sliced (optional)
- ½ cup white sugar
- ½ tablespoon baking powder
- 1 teaspoon vanilla extract
- 7 ounces canned sweetened condensed milk
- ½ cup whipped cream (optional)

Method:

1. Grease a small square or rectangular baking dish with a little cooking spray and set aside.
2. Add whites into a mixing bowl. Beat with an electric mixer on high speed until stiff peaks are formed.
3. Add sugar and beat until the mixture is shiny.
4. Add yolks, one at a time and beat well each time.
5. Lower the speed of the electric mixer to medium speed. Add flour, 1 tablespoon at a time and beat well each time.
6. Add baking powder, vanilla, evaporated milk, condensed milk and milk and beat well.

7. Transfer the batter into the baking dish.
8. Bake in a preheated oven at 350° F for about 20 – 30 minutes. A toothpick, when inserted in the center, should come out clean. Do not open the oven for 20 - 25 minutes.
9. Remove the cake from the oven and cool for 15 minutes.
10. Meanwhile, add cream, evaporated milk and condensed milk into a blender and blend until smooth. Pour over the cake. Spread it evenly.
11. Chill the cake for a couple of hours. Cut into 6 equal pieces.
12. Serve with whipped cream and strawberries.

Avocado Ice Cream

Serves: 4

Nutritional values per serving:

Calories – 224, Fat – 6 g, Carbohydrate – 38 g, Protein – 1 g

Ingredients:

- ¾ cup ripe avocado puree
- 2/3 cup sugar
- ¾ cup water
- 3 tablespoons tequila
- 2 tablespoons lime juice
- 1 teaspoon lime zest, grated to garnish

Method:

1. Add avocado puree, water, sugar, lime juice and tequila into the food processor and blend until smooth.
2. Transfer into a bowl. Cover with cling wrap and chill for at least an hour.
3. Pour the mixture into the ice cream maker and churn the ice cream according the manufacturer's instructions or freeze in the freezer for about 4 hours.

Scoop into bowls and serve garnished with lime zest.

Apple Enchilada Dessert

Serves: 3

Nutritional values per serving:

Calories – 484, Fat – 13.5 g, Carbohydrate – 88.3 g, Protein – 4.5 g

Ingredients:

- ½ can apple pie filling (from a 21 ounces can)
- ½ teaspoon ground cinnamon + extra to top
- ¼ cup white sugar
- ¼ cup water
- 3 flour tortillas (8 inches each)
- 2 ½ tablespoons margarine
- ¼ cup packed brown sugar

Method:

1. Spread the tortillas on the countertop,
2. Divide the apple pie filling among the tortillas. Spread it evenly. Sprinkle cinnamon on top.
3. Roll and place in a greased baking dish with the seam side facing down.
4. Add sugar, margarine and water into a saucepan. Place the saucepan over medium low heat. Stir constantly for 2-3 minutes until the sugar dissolves completely.
5. Pour over the tortillas. Sprinkle some more cinnamon.
6. Bake in a preheated oven at 350° F for about 20 minutes.

Conclusion

I would like to thank you once again for purchasing this book.

In recent times, Mexican cuisine has steadily gained popularity. It is a fusion of traditional South American and European food, and therefore it is quite exciting. Not only is it exciting cuisine, but traditional Mexican food is quite healthy too.

Mexican cuisine is vibrant, exciting and flavorful and is a mixture of local ingredients. Fortunately for us, the ingredients that you need to cook Mexican food are easily available at most of your local markets. With the help of this cookbook, you can cook your version of truly delightful Mexican dishes in your kitchen! Mexican cooking is popular for the rich flavors it seamlessly incorporates in every dish. The general impression of Mexican cuisine is that of spicy, heavy and fatty food. After looking at the recipes in this book, you will realize that Mexican cuisine is anything but that. It is all about using fresh and seasonal ingredients to cook a delicious meal. The common impression of Mexican food that we have is due to commercialization of this cuisine. There is so much more to Mexican food than just tacos and nachos.

The recipes that are mentioned in this book are flavorful, nutritious and pack quite a punch. Mexican cooking will no longer seem intimidating to you. Once you understand the different flavor combinations, you can experiment with the ingredients. Mexican meals are all about bold flavors, so don't hold back and learn to have some fun with flavors in the kitchen.

The next time you have your friends or family over for a meal, you can cook a traditional three-course Mexican meal for them! That does sound quite wonderful, doesn't it? Perhaps you can whip up a tasty Mexican meal at home the next time you crave for some Mexican food. All that you need to do to cook tasty food is gather the necessary ingredients and follow the simple recipes given in this book. The recipes curated in this book are quite simple to understand and easy to follow. You no longer have to slave away in the kitchen for hours on end and can cook tasty food within no time at all. Make sure that you stock your pantry with the ingredients you need and you are good to go.

Finally, if you enjoyed this book then I'd like to ask you for a favor. Will you be kind enough to leave a review for this book on Amazon? It would be greatly appreciated!

Thank you and good luck!

Other Books by Grizzly Publishing

"Jamaican Cookbook: Traditional Jamaican Recipes Made Easy"

https://www.amazon.com/dp/B07B68KL8D

"Brazilian Instant Pot Cookbook: Delicious Pressure Cooked Meals Made Fast and Easy"

https://www.amazon.com/dp/B078XBYP89

"Norwegian Cookbook: Traditional Scandinavian Recipes Made Easy"

https://www.amazon.com/dp/B079M2W223

"Casserole Cookbook: Delicious Casserole Recipes From Around The World"

https://www.amazon.com/dp/B07B6GV61Q